Prairie Dogs

Prairie Dogs

by Dorothy Hinshaw Patent
photographs by William Muñoz

CLARION BOOKS · NEW YORK

The author wishes to thank Dr. Daniel Uresk of the
Rocky Mountain Forest and Range Experimental Station,
U.S. Forest Service, for reading and
commenting on the manuscript.

Clarion Books
a Houghton Mifflin Company imprint
215 Park Avenue South, New York, NY 10003
Text copyright © 1993 by Dorothy Hinshaw Patent
Photographs copyright © 1993 by William Muñoz

The photographs on pages 16, 53, and 54, by LuRay Parker, are
used with the permission of the Wyoming Game and Fish Department.
Printed in Italy.
Book design by Carol Goldenberg.

Library of Congress Cataloging-in-Publication Data
Patent, Dorothy Hinshaw.
Prairie dogs / by Dorothy Hinshaw Patent : photographs by
William Muñoz.
p.   cm
Includes bibliographical references (p. 59) and index.
Summary: Discusses the habits and life cycle of prairie dogs and
examines their place in the ecology of their grassland environment.
ISBN 0-395-56572-3
1. Prairie dogs—Juvenile literature. 2. Prairie dogs—Ecology—
Juvenile literature. [1. Prairie dogs. 2. Prairie ecology.
3. Ecology.] I. Muñoz, William, ill. II. Title.
QL737.R68P38 1993
599.32'32—dc20
92-34724   CIP   AC

NWI 10 9 8 7 6 5 4 3 2 1

To Sean, champion rattlesnake finder

Contents

CHAPTER ONE

A Very Social Squirrel

The morning air is cool over the prairie when the first furry head peeks out from the deep dark burrow. The prairie dog looks to the left and then to the right, focusing her shiny black eyes near and far, checking for danger. Then she disappears again underground. A few minutes later she comes back. This time, after one more careful check, she crawls out over the mound of earth surrounding the hole in the ground. The cinnamon-brown fur covering her chunky body shines in the bright sunlight. Within minutes, her four pups stream out of the burrow. Soon the family is surrounded by activity. Nearby, a group of pups race about and tumble in play. All around, prairie dogs are nibbling on grass. They nip off the blades near the base, then hold them with their front feet as they eat.

Prairie dogs are not dogs. They were given this name because of their barklike warning call. It may be hard to believe

Black-tailed prairie dog.

at first, but prairie dogs are actually rodents — a kind of squirrel. The squirrels most familiar to us run along tree branches and stop to sit with their long, bushy tails curved up behind them. They are generally solitary animals, except during mating and when a female is raising a family. But prairie dogs never climb trees — they often live in places

Prairie dogs spend a lot of time eating.

where no trees can even be seen. Their stubby tails are covered with short fur. Their bodies are stout, not sleek and slim like those of their tree-dwelling cousins. An adult gray tree squirrel weighs about 1⅓ pounds; a black-tailed prairie dog weighs 2 to 3 pounds. Unlike their solitary relatives, prairie dogs live in large colonies called towns instead of all alone.

No one knows how big a prairie dog town can get. In 1901, a government biologist estimated that a series of towns he found in Texas covered 25,000 square miles — more than the states of Connecticut, Massachusetts, New Hampshire, and Rhode Island combined — and could have been home to 400

A prairie dog town.

million black-tailed prairie dogs, by far the most common species. Scientists call the black-tailed prairie dog *Cynomys ludovicianus*. At one time, as many as 5 billion prairie dogs lived in North America.

Prairie dogs live only on North American grasslands. Three

People have covered most of the prairie with highways, farms, pastures, and towns.

types of prairie once covered the Great Plains all the way from southern Canada across the United States into northern Mexico. In the east, where there was more rainfall, tallgrass prairie was dominant. Tallgrasses may grow up to six feet in height. In the west, where the land was drier, shortgrasses grew. In between the tallgrass and shortgrass prairies grew a mixed grass combination. Today, most of the prairie is gone, converted into cities, farmland, and pastures. But bits of it still survive here and there.

Prairie dogs don't live on the tallgrass prairie, where enemies can easily hide and where heavy rains might flood their burrows. They favor the dry shortgrass prairies and areas of mixed grass. There, by constantly trimming the plants with their sharp teeth, prairie dogs are able to maintain their own areas of shortgrass.

Fortunately, stretches of prairie still remain.

A white-tailed prairie dog. Photo by LuRay Parker.

Black-tailed prairie dogs are highly social.

There are five kinds of prairie dogs. The black-tailed prairie dog once inhabited the entire midsection of North America, ranging all the way from southern Saskatchewan through the Great Plains states into northern Mexico. In the west, it lived up to the base of the Rocky Mountains. The tallgrass prairie limited its range to the east.

The white-tailed prairie dog lives in smaller colonies than does the black-tailed species. It is found in the west central part of the prairie, from south central Montana through western Wyoming into northeastern Utah and northwestern Colorado. The rare Utah prairie dog lives only in south central

Utah, while Gunnison's prairie dog inhabits the plains south of the white-tails and on into Arizona and western New Mexico. The Mexican prairie dog inhabits northeastern Mexico.

Life in a Town

In addition to being the most common species, the black-tailed prairie dog is also the most social. Each individual has its place in the family, and each family plays a role in the life of the colony. Just like a human city, a black-tailed prairie dog town is organized. Towns may be divided up into smaller sections called wards. The wards are separated from one another by trees, streams, hills, or other natural features. Within a ward, prairie dogs live in small family groups called coteries. Each coterie consists of one adult male, from one to six (usually three or four) adult females, their year-old offspring, and new young of the season. Members of the coterie share a burrow system that covers about 0.6 acre.

Like other rodents such as mice, prairie dogs have plenty of enemies. Their burrows provide some protection from predators. But living in a town helps just as much. With many eyes, ears, and noses constantly attentive to potential danger, these wary animals are rarely caught by surprise.

Prairie dogs keep vegetation short within the town, nipping off plants that can interfere with a clear view or provide cover for predators. Their feeding also keeps the grass short, giving the town the look of a giant lawn pitted with burrows.

Coyotes sometimes feed on unwary prairie dogs.

This prairie dog is nipping off a plant that could block its view.

When a prairie dog leaves the nest to feed, it comes out slowly, looking this way and that to check for danger. If all seems clear, the animal will emerge. While they are outside their burrows, prairie dogs are always on the alert for any strange sight, sound, or smell. If one senses danger, it gives a barklike warning call, its black-tipped tail vibrating with each bark. When they hear the warning bark, all the other prairie dogs within earshot pay attention and are ready to

When a prairie dog senses possible danger, it gives a warning bark that alerts its neighbors.

flee. Within seconds, they can dash for the safety of their burrows.

Golden eagles, various large hawks, rattlesnakes, coyotes, and badgers are the main enemies of prairie dogs. Most of them can be easily foiled by a quick dive into a burrow. Only the badger, with its powerful claws, can dig prairie dogs out. Rattlesnakes can hunt by crawling into the burrows and eating young pups.

A rattlesnake waits at a burrow entrance.

Mound entrance to a burrow.

The Burrow Environment

A prairie dog burrow is a carefully built, complicated network of twelve to a hundred feet of tunnels and rooms. The tunnels are about five inches in diameter. The burrow usually has two entrances, sometimes three. One entrance slants downward from a low mound of earth perhaps five feet in diameter. This is the end from which the tunnel was originally dug. The other entrance plunges straight downward and is topped by a craterlike mound as tall as three feet. The two entrances are shaped by the animals. The mound is made by arranging the material dug out while tunneling. The crater entrance starts as a ring of soil, uprooted plants,

Crater burrow entrance.

Prairie dogs are energetic diggers.

24

and surface litter. After the first rain following tunnel building, the animals use their noses to compact the moist material of the crater. As time goes by, more soil is added and packed around the crater, making the cone of soil taller. Sometimes, burrow entrances are flat, with no mound or crater.

A prairie dog moves dirt to help shape a burrow.

A young prairie dog peeks out to see if it is safe to leave the burrow.

At the crater end, there is often an enlargement of the tunnel three to five feet underground. A prairie dog can turn around in this space and return to the surface easily. After diving into the tunnel to escape danger, the animal may wait in this area, sometimes chattering at a frustrated enemy on the surface.

The main room in a burrow is the nesting chamber, an enlargement of the tunnel about the size of a basketball. This is where the animals sleep at night. The floor of the nesting chamber is covered with a two-inch layer of dry grass. There are also side pockets in the burrow, some empty, some filled with stored food. Parts of the burrow containing dead prairie dogs may be blocked off with plugs of dirt. Air circulates inside, entering from the mound entrance and leaving through the crater.

The burrows help moderate the harsh climate of the Great Plains. While the summer daytime temperature above ground ranges from 77 to 99 degrees Fahrenheit, the temperature inside the burrows fluctuates only between 80 and 89 degrees. In late December, it may be 25 degrees outside, but the burrows get no colder than 42 degrees. The humidity inside is high, which helps keep the animals from losing too much water from their bodies. This is a danger in a dry environment where drinking water is rare or nonexistent and prairie dogs must get enough water from their food to meet their needs.

CHAPTER TWO

Family Life

The prairie dogs' complex system of burrows not only protects them from enemies and from the elements, it also shields much of their lives from the curious eyes of scientists. Because they spend so much of their time underground, we can only guess at certain aspects of prairie dog life. We don't know, for example, how much time the animals spend feeding or sleeping while in their burrows.

During the winter, prairie dogs do not go into hibernation. Instead, they fatten up in the fall by eating as much as possible. The fat helps insulate them from the cold and is slowly utilized over the winter to provide energy when it is too cold or stormy to go outside to look for something to eat. Prairie dogs also store food in their burrows to eat during the winter.

Prairie dogs come out of their burrows during the winter when the weather permits.

During the warmer months, prairie dogs put on fat for the winter.

Starting a New Family

In late winter (March in South Dakota), black-tailed prairie dogs begin to breed. The season lasts only about two weeks. Mating takes place underground. The female keeps to herself after she has mated. She chooses a burrow for giving birth and chases other animals away if they come too close.

The pups — usually four or five, but sometimes as many as ten — are born thirty to thirty-five days later. For the first five or six weeks of their lives, the young prairie dogs remain underground, protected in the burrow from most of their possible enemies. The pups are tiny at birth, weighing a little more than half an ounce each, but they grow fast feeding on their mother's milk. By the time they leave the burrow, they weigh about eight times as much as when they were born. While the pups are still in the burrow, their mother stays with them most of the time. She comes out to feed perhaps 25 percent of the daylight hours. The other adult coterie members are outside 90 percent of the day.

Recently, scientists have discovered a strange thing about black-tailed prairie dogs. The females in a coterie are generally sisters. Yet one female may sneak into her neighbor's burrow while she is away and kill the pups, even eating some of them. This behavior seems strange in such a social animal. No one knows for sure why females kill pups, but it seems to be a common occurrence. Despite the fact that predators are only rarely able to attack pups in the nest, about half never appear above ground. Most of them were probably killed by female prairie dogs.

Young pups are cautious about leaving their burrow.

Once they are old enough to come out, the pups begin to eat plants.

When the young animals that survive infancy do venture outside, they are ready to feed themselves, although they still take some milk for another week or so. Once they are able to leave the burrows, the youngsters are tolerated and protected by all members of the coterie. A female may even nurse another's pups. The pups follow the adults about, pestering them for attention. They run and tussle with one another in play.

Like other young animals, prairie dog pups play together.

Like other social animals, prairie dogs communicate with each other in a variety of ways. The warning bark alerts them to possible danger. The hawk warning bark is a more intense, higher-pitched warning bark. When prairie dogs hear the hawk warning nearby, they dash for their burrows without hesitation.

Prairie dogs have a special way of declaring their coterie

When danger threatens, prairie dogs run quickly to the safety of their burrow.

A prairie dog giving a territorial call.

territories. Now and then, one of the animals will suddenly throw itself upright, standing on its hind legs with its head thrown back, nose pointed toward the sky. A two-note call is part of this display. The first sound is made as the animal goes up, the other as it comes down.

Besides their territorial display and warning bark, prairie dogs also communicate through smell and touch. Whenever two animals meet, they come together with their mouths open and "kiss." If they are from the same coterie and recognize each other, they part quietly and go on their own ways. But if one is outside its own territory, the two animals crouch on their bellies, wagging their tails as they crawl toward each other. The individual that doesn't belong generally gives up and flees without a fight.

Friendly relations are also maintained through mutual grooming. The animals clean one another's coats by nibbling with their teeth. The pups are especially eager to be groomed, often begging adults to groom them by crawling under their bodies or following them around.

Coterie members "kiss" when they meet.

When prairie dogs from different coteries meet, they do so cautiously.

Male prairie dogs are very watchful.

Life and Death

Female prairie dogs may mate when they are only a year old or wait until they are two. A female may live for seven years and usually spends all that time in the same coterie. Males, on the other hand, are not likely to survive more than five years. Their lives are more stressful, for they are most responsible for protecting the coterie from invasion by other prairie dogs. The dominant male is always watchful, sitting on rocks or burrow craters to make sure no strange prairie dogs enter his territory. If they do, they are challenged and usually leave quickly. If a young invading male senses that the dominant male is old or weak, however, he may keep coming back until he succeeds in taking over the coterie.

Male prairie dogs need to leave the coterie in order to breed. At about the same time the pups emerge in the spring,

New coteries are set up around the edges of prosperous towns.

yearling males are likely to leave their families and move to the edge of the colony. There, they attempt to establish their own coteries. Females of different ages may also move, though this is less common. Adventurous individuals of both sexes are more likely to be killed by predators than are animals living safely within the town. Around the edges there are fewer eyes and ears alert for danger. There are also likely to be more tall plants that can hide enemies.

Most of the time, the restless animals that leave their coteries go no farther than the outer reaches of their own town. Through their settlements, the town can grow rapidly when there is enough food and few enemies. Some animals, however, are real wanderers and may stray as far as seven miles from home. When these individuals survive, they can establish new towns.

CHAPTER THREE

Prairie Dogs and Cattle

Large prairie dog towns once dotted the entire Great Plains region of mixed and shortgrass prairie. But today, these social squirrels live only here and there. Their numbers have been reduced by about 90 percent. As with so many other animals, habitat loss is part of the reason for the decline in numbers. Farms, highways, and cities now occupy what were once prairie dog towns. But there is a bigger reason for their decline. The prairies where bison once roamed are now the domain of cattle. Prairie dogs and cows both eat grass, so ranchers look upon prairie dogs as competitors for their livestock's food and try to exterminate them.

———— Poisoning Prairie Dogs ————

At the turn of the century, biologist C. Hart Merriam, chief of the U.S. Biological Survey, calculated that 256 prairie dogs would eat the same amount of grass as one cow. Scientists now put this figure at about 300 instead of 256. Merriam concluded that eliminating these rodents would allow more cattle to be raised. The government stepped in to help get rid of prairie dogs, poisoning them by the thousands all across the plains.

Grass is a favorite prairie dog food.

Nowadays, little prairie remains that is not inhabited by cattle or other livestock.

In recent years, scientists have studied the ecology of prairie dog towns and the policy of poisoning. They reached some surprising conclusions. Killing prairie dogs may make ranchers feel they're being helped, but the costs involved outweigh any possible benefit. For example, from 1980 to 1984, the Bureau of Indian Affairs (a branch of the federal government) spent $6.2 million poisoning prairie dogs on about 450,000 acres of the Pine Ridge Indian Reservation in South Dakota. The land itself isn't worth that much. The cost of the poisoning also exceeded the value of the livestock it was meant to aid. Besides, poisoning prairie dogs is not an especially effective treatment. After a town has been poisoned out, it can be rapidly repopulated from nearby colonies. Within three years, the town can be back to its original population, if many cattle are left out to graze. However, if the numbers of cattle are reduced and the vegetation grows back taller than 6 inches, prairie dog return is much slower.

Prairie dogs eat more than just grass.

Despite the cost and the frequent ineffectiveness of poisoning, the practice continues. During 1985 and 1986, another 225,000 acres on the Pine Ridge Reservation were poisoned out, at a cost of several million dollars. Prairie dogs are even killed where there are no cattle: they have been poisoned in two national parks in South Dakota because the National Farm Bureau won a suit against the National Park Service, forcing it to use poison on prairie dogs within the parks.

Are these social creatures really such an economic drain on the cattle industry? If the results of recent studies can be generalized, the answer is probably no. Prairie dogs tend to thrive where cattle have grazed away tallgrasses, so their populations increase after cattle have been out on the land. But they don't necessarily eat the same food as the cows. Some of the plants prairie dogs prefer are not considered to be good cattle forage, though others are. No one has yet proved that prairie dogs consume more than 7 percent of the available food, even on large towns.

Some people would say that Manning Corral Prairie Dog Town is "infested" with prairie dogs.

Even though eliminating prairie dogs is costly, and even though scientists are beginning to doubt that these animals deprive cattle of feed, prairie dogs are still considered pests in most of the Great Plains states. Areas that are home to prairie dog towns are likely to be termed "infested." In some counties, a person can be forced to get rid of prairie dogs on his land if a neighbor complains about them.

Prairie Dogs and Bison

Understanding how prairie dogs interact with cattle requires some knowledge of prairie natural history. Prairie dogs and bison evolved to share the prairie over thousands and thousands of years, before farmers and ranchers claimed the land. The two species live in harmony, actually helping each other by means of their feeding habits. Bison prefer to graze on grasses growing in prairie dog towns where the prairie dogs feed rather than on the open prairie. Even though the grass is kept short and is constantly grazed, both the rodents and the bison thrive.

Why is this so? Scientists have studied the chemical

Bison prefer grazing around the edges of prairie dog towns.

The grass is kept short in a prairie dog town.

Cattle are often restricted to certain pastures by fences.

makeup of the plants that the bison and prairie dogs feed on. They have found that the grasses that are continually clipped short by the animals have an especially high content of nitrogen, the most important nutrient in the plants benefitting both bison and prairie dogs. Grass that gets tall has less nitrogen.

Today, cattle take the place of bison in the prairie community over most of the Great Plains. Cattle are close relatives of bison, and live in much the same way, so one would expect that they should be able to get along fine with prairie dogs. When scientists compared the market weights of cattle that grazed on a prairie dog town with those of cattle grazing elsewhere, they found that the cattle weighed about the same. The prairie dogs didn't significantly deprive the cattle of their feed, despite Merriam's turn-of-the-century estimates.

One important difference between cattle and bison can affect the health of the prairie. Bison are migratory, grazing intensively in an area and then moving on, often not returning for months or even years. Cattle, however, are left in the same area for long periods of time. For this reason, it is important not to put out too many cattle that might overgraze and damage the range, even if no prairie dogs are present.

CHAPTER FOUR

Prairies and Prairie Dogs

Bison aren't the only animals attracted to prairie dog towns. These areas of short grass and disturbed ground provide a variety of habitats used by everything from insects to eagles. Prairie dogs churn up and mix the soil, loosening it with their digging and fertilizing it with their droppings. The plant material they take into their burrows and the bodies of prairie dogs that die underground also increase the soil's fertility.

Prairie dog towns support a greater diversity of life than the surrounding undisturbed prairie. Forty percent of western wildlife species are associated with prairie dog colonies. In western South Dakota, that means thirty-six kinds of mammals, eighty-eight birds, six reptiles, and four amphibians as well as spiders, insects, and other invertebrates.

The rough-legged hawk is a common resident of prairie dog towns.

Meadowlarks often make their homes in the towns.

Pronghorn antelope feed in the interior of prairie dog towns, where plants other than grasses often grow. Like the grasses, the other plants are kept clipped by the prairie dogs and have a high nitrogen content, providing the pronghorn with quality feed. The antelope may benefit as well from the efficient prairie dog alarm system that warns of approaching predators.

Abandoned burrows provide shelter from the hot summer sun and bitter winter cold for dozens of creatures. Burrowing owls nest there, while salamanders and insects find a moist, protected environment in the dark tunnels. Prairie rattlesnakes gather in the burrows for the winter, as do box turtles, lizards, and spadefoot toads.

Pronghorn frequent the centers of the towns.

Red foxes as well as swift foxes may be found in a prairie dog town.

Above ground, swift foxes, which feed on prairie dogs and insects, tend to settle within a half mile of towns, while horned larks and killdeer nest inside towns. Other rodents, like deer mice and grasshopper mice, also take advantage of the town habitat. Many bird species whose numbers have declined since the 1960s favor life in the dog town — mountain plovers, Cassin's sparrows, and lark buntings, for example.

The Black-Footed Ferret

One reason why scientific attention has begun to focus on prairie dogs is concern about the endangered black-footed ferret. This predator is highly specialized, living only on prairie dog towns and feeding almost exclusively on prairie dogs. Once thought to be extinct, black-footed ferrets turned up in a dog town in Wyoming in the mid-1980s. Scientists were afraid that the animals would die out, so during the winter of 1986–87, they trapped the few remaining ferrets. Since then, the ferrets have been bred in the safety of captivity.

The breeding program has been so successful that by the

The black-footed ferret, with its slim body, is well designed for traveling through prairie dog burrows. Photo by LuRay Parker / © 1985 Wyoming Game & Fish Dept.

Black-footed ferrets are active, alert predators. Photo by LuRay Parker /
© 1985 Wyoming Game & Fish Dept.

fall of 1991, forty-nine ferrets were returned to the wild on white-tailed prairie dog towns in the largest prairie dog area of Wyoming. No one knew if these captive-bred animals could survive in the wild. During the winter, scientists returned to find seven to nine ferrets still in the area. Others had wandered away, perhaps to live nearby. When they checked again in the summer of 1992, the scientists were delighted to find two mother ferrets with litters of young and at least three other adults. Not only could the animals survive, they could breed in the wild.

In the fall of 1992, a hundred more ferrets were released in the same area. Future plans include release at other sites, including the area near Meeteetse, Wyoming, from which the last wild ferrets were removed. Five or six sites in Arizona, Colorado, Montana, and South Dakota are also on the list. Each release area must be no smaller than 6000 acres, large enough to support about fifty ferrets.

Big areas of prairie, like this one, are needed as homes for black-footed ferrets.

Prairies are home to wildflowers as well as grasses.

Since black-footed ferrets live only in prairie dog towns, concern for their survival includes concern for their prairie dog prey. Without large numbers of prairie dogs spread out over many miles of prairie, the ferrets will not be able to survive in the wild. The rescue of the black-footed ferret from extinction means preservation of patches of prairie, the home for so many of our wild species.

Saving the Prairie

Fortunately for prairie dogs and other grassland residents, interest in habitat preservation and restoration has increased recently across the country. In earlier years, when governments set aside parklands, they chose places with beautiful mountains or huge trees. Landscapes that appealed to people seemed most important. Now we realize that it is just as important to preserve all kinds of natural habitats, not only those that are most dramatic to the human eye. Across the Great Plains, bits of original prairie are being found and preserved, and the original prairie vegetation is being encouraged to grow where it has been crowded out by nonnative plants, allowing the prairies to regenerate.

Fortunately, the usefulness of the prairie dog and the habitat this animal creates is appreciated more and more. We can hope that government poisoning programs will be sharply cut and that these animals can be left in peace, helping to keep our prairies closer to their natural state and saving the homes of dozens of unique American plants and animals along with the prairie dogs.

Selected Bibliography

This list contains some of the references consulted during work on this book. Students will find the starred (*) references particularly helpful.

Agnew, William, Daniel W. Uresk, and Richard M. Hansen. "Flora and Fauna Associated with Prairie Dog Colonies and Adjacent Ungrazed Mixed-grass Prairie in Western South Dakota." *Journal of Range Management* 39 (1986): 135–38.

*Chadwick, Douglas. "Rescuing Our Rarest Prairie Predator." *Defenders* 66 (March/April 1991): 10–23.

Cincotta, R. P. "Note on Mound Architecture of the Black-tailed Prairie Dog." *Great Basin Naturalist* 49 (1989): 621–23.

Collins, Alan R., John P. Workman, and Daniel W. Uresk. "An Economic Analysis of Black-tailed Prairie Dog [Cynomys ludovicianus] Control." *Journal of Range Management* 37 (1984): 358–61.

Garrett, Monte G., and William L. Franklin. "Behavioral Ecology of Dispersal in the Black-tailed Prairie Dog." *Journal of Mammology* 69 (1988): 236–50.

*Grossmann, John. "A Prairie Dog Companion." *Audubon* (March 1987): 53–67.

*Gunderson, Harvey L. "Under and Around a Prairie Dog Town." *Natural History* 88 (October 1978): 57–67.

Holland, E. A., and J. K. Detling. "Plant Response to Herbivory and Belowground Nitrogen Cycling." *Ecology* 71 (1990): 1040–49.

Hoogland, J. L. "The Evolution of Coloniality in White-tailed and Black-tailed Prairie Dogs (Sciuridae: Cynomys leucurus and C. ludovicianus)." *Ecology* 62 (1981): 252–72.

Jones, J. Knox, Jr., et al. *Mammals of the Northern Great Plains.* Lincoln, NB: University of Nebraska Press, 1983.

King, John A. "Social Behavior, Social Organization, and Population Dynamics in a Black-Tailed Prairiedog [sic] Town in the Black Hills of South Dakota." *Contributions from the Laboratory of Vertebrate Biology, University of Michigan* 67 (April, 1955).

Miller, B., et al. "A Proposal to Conserve Black-footed Ferrets and the Prairie Dog Ecosystem." *Environmental Management* 14 (1990): 763–70.

Nowak, Ronald M. *Walker's Mammals of the World.* 5th ed. Baltimore, MD: The Johns Hopkins Press, 1991.

Sharps, J. C., and D. W. Uresk. "Ecological Review of Black-tailed Prairie Dogs and Associated Species in Western South Dakota." *Great Basin Naturalist* 50 (1990): 339–46.

Stockrahm, Donna M. Bruns, and Robert W. Seabloom. "Comparative Reproductive Performance of Black-tailed Prairie Dog Populations in North Dakota." *Journal of Mammology* 69 (1988): 160–64.

Index

ABOUT THE AUTHOR AND PHOTOGRAPHER

DOROTHY HINSHAW PATENT holds a Ph.D. in zoology from the University of California at Berkeley. She has written more than seventy books for children and young adults on wildlife and wildlife management, most recently *Ospreys*. In 1987, Dr. Patent received the Eva L. Gordon Award for Children's Science Literature for the body of her work. She and her husband, Gregory Patent, have two grown sons. They live in Missoula, Montana.

WILLIAM MUÑOZ earned his B.A. degree in history from the University of Montana. He has collaborated with Dorothy Hinshaw Patent on many successful photo essays, including *Ospreys*. He lives with his wife, Sandy, and son, Sean, in St. Ignatius, Montana, where he divides his time between freelance photography and gardening.